Rating Your
Dating
While
Waiting
for Mating

Rating Your Dating While Waiting for Mating

ED YOUNG

Creality Publishing
Dallas, Texas

RATING YOUR DATING WHILE WAITING FOR MATING

Ed Young

Published in Dallas, TX by Creality Publishing.

CONTENTS

1 PRE-NUPTIAL NURSERY RHYMES 1
Moving from Fanciful Rhyme to Biblical Reason

2 THE ULTI-MATE RIDE 29
Fixing the Flaws of Defective Dating

3 CHECKS AND BALANCES 53
*Reading and Heeding the Warning Signs
in a Relationship*

4 DANGEROUS BINDS 77
Maintaining Purity in the Midst of Passion

CHAPTER

1

∞∞

PRE-NUPTIAL NURSERY RHYMES

*Moving from Fanciful Rhyme
to Biblical Reason*

My mother loves nursery rhymes. Name any of the big ones, *Old King Cole, Jack Sprat, There Was An Old Woman Who Lived in a Shoe*, and she can recite them right off the top of her head. During the first forty-eight months of my life, she repeated these nursery rhymes to me over and over again, before bedtime, nap time, mealtime, any time.

As a kid, I bought into these rhymes. However, as I matured, I came to the realization that these rhymes were made up, orchestrated by someone with a very creative mind.

I don't have any illusions when reading about a political figure named Old King Cole. I don't think that

I will ever be driving down a freeway and look to my left and see an old woman who lives in a shoe. They are phony, false, just for children.

However, many of us are still reciting nursery rhymes and believing them. Men and woman in the throes of premarital bliss say pre-nuptial nursery rhymes as they walk down the carpeted aisle in holy matrimony.

Before I jump on that train and get more into the rhymes we believe, let me throttle back a little bit and share a couple of facts with you. A *USA Today* poll reveals that 49 percent of adults in America today are not married; they are currently single. Sixty-four percent of those who are currently single have never been married, 22 percent are divorced or separated, and the rest are either widowed or living with a partner.

It's clear that a lot of singles out there are looking for the love of their life, but too many of them are running into failure and disappointment. According to a recent study from the federal government, more than two-fifths (43 percent) of first marriages end in either divorce or separation within fifteen years.

Many marriages today are not lasting because couples are not doing the work they need to do before they reach the altar. God's resources for a lasting marriage begin long before you say "I do;" therefore, it's critical that singles understand the fine art of spouse selection.

Next to the decision to follow Christ, your choice of whom you will marry is the most important earthly decision you will ever make. And the best way to enhance your marriage for the long haul is to do the necessary work before the wedding day.

As I share with you these Pre-nuptial Nursery Rhymes, I want you to think about how these impact life and relationships. Whether you're a single adult searching for the right person to marry, a student who is just in the "going out" phase of life, or a single or married parent thinking about the future of your children, you need to understand the vicious cycle of fanciful rhymes that many of us have learned and continue to recite in our relationships.

The media encourages us to repeat these rhymes. Pressure from our culture causes us to do it. But make no mistake, these nursery rhymes are not just innocent kid's stuff. They will mess you up.

My desire for this chapter, and this book, is that it will cause you to take a step back and understand the reality of marriage and how high the stakes are before you make the critical decision to marry someone.

THE HICKORY DICKORY DOCK DANCE

Let's look at the first nursery rhyme that we repeat:

Hickory dickory dock,
the mouse ran up the clock.
The clock struck one,
the mouse ran down.
Hickory dickory dock.

Hickory dickory dock, the old biological clock begins to tick, drowning out reason and common sense for both men and women. Women just want those little ones; it's that maternal instinct. And men would love to have a chip off the old block—someone they could throw a football with. This causes us to be like the proverbial mouse.

WE GET MARRIED JUST FOR THE SAKE OF GETTING MARRIED, WITHOUT REALLY CONSIDERING WHETHER OR NOT WE'RE MARRYING THE RIGHT PERSON.

We become all freaky and frenzied about the ticking of the clock, run down the carpeted aisle to get hooked up. We get married just for the sake of getting married, without really considering whether or not we're marrying the right person.

Peer Pressure Cooker

This pressure to do the hickory dickory dock dance starts when we are little kids playing dress-up with Ken and Barbie. It intensifies as people begin to ask us to be involved in their weddings, as a groomsman or a bridesmaid. Giddy girls rush up to us, their ring finger at eye level, showing us their relational rock. Friends ask them, "Oh, how did he ask you?" or "How many carets is that?"

And a subtle form of competition begins. We don't really talk about this competitive urge, but turning over and over on the rotisserie grills of our minds are thoughts of beating the next person to the alter, of having a bigger ring, and of having an even more romantic proposal story for our friends to "ooh" and "awe" over.

With the increasing pressure to marry, singles begin to see married people and feel that they are glaring at them. They feel those married people are singing songs to them under their breath, like "What's wrong with you? What's wrong with you? Life will have no meaning until you say, 'I do.'" They see themselves at wedding receptions trying to get that elusive garter or the bouquet. They begin to feel like unclaimed pieces of luggage left at the airport.

You would think that parents would identify with them, that they could relate. But parents drop these subtle hints, more like bombs. "When are we going to have a daughter-in-law?" "I sure would like to have some grandchildren running around the house some day. You know, we aren't getting any younger." Parents should know better than to pressure their kids into marriage, yet many continue to lay it on thick. And it causes singles and students to say, "Hickory dickory dock. The mouse ran up the clock, and I am going to run down the wedding runner. I have got to get married."

The Time Factor

But the relational rush has a bad track record. Kansas State University conducted a study that showed a direct correlation between the length of a courtship and marital satisfaction. Dating is a lease with an option to buy, and most leases run for several years. That is why I challenge you, again, to wait at least a year before you get married.

When our twins were learning to read, they pronounced every syllable, every letter very deliberately. Take a hint from them. Singles, take your T...I...M...E....

"T" stands for temperament. Date someone long enough to see his or her true temperament. What's their temper like? How do they handle stress and conflict?

"I" stands for integrity. We get the word integrity from integer, which means a whole number. During a quick courtship, too many of us are just giving out fractions, putting our best foot forward and only revealing our best side. With time comes knowledge of the whole person and all the sides—good, bad, and ugly.

"M" is for maturity. Is this person mature? I'm not talking about chronological age but real growth and maturity. Are they ready for the responsibility and commitment of marriage?

"E" represents enjoyment. Does this relationship put wind in your sail? Is this individual a friend? Do you really enjoy spending time talking to them and sharing activities together?

Six Months to Life

"Well, Ed, what if I wait too long? What if I burn up a year and then get married and discover that I could have gotten married six months earlier. I've wasted time." No, you haven't. Who cares that you dated the person you end up marrying a few months longer? This is a much better scenario than getting married six months sooner to the wrong person and regretting it the rest of your life. Six additional months of waiting and anticipation is a small price to pay compared to a potential lifetime of regret.

REFUSE TO DO THE HICKORY DICKORY DOCK DANCE, BECAUSE A RODENT-LIKE MENTALITY DOES NOT WORK IN MARRIAGE

Please honor God's covenant of marriage enough to give yourself and your potential mate some time. Let the shine wear off and take your T...I...M...E....Refuse to do the Hickory Dickory Dock dance, because a rodent-like mentality does not work in marriage.

Humpty Dumpty Thinking

Pre-nuptial nursery rhyme number two goes like this:

> *Humpty Dumpty sat on a wall.*
> *Humpty Dumpty had a great fall.*
> *All the king's horses and all the king's men*
> *couldn't put Humpty together again.*

Are you a Humpty Dumpter? Humpty Dumpty found out that it isn't easy being oval. Humpty Dumpters have this line of thinking, "If I get married, get hooked up with this special someone, they can fix my fractured life. They can put a cast around me and heal my brokenness."

Record numbers of us are emerging from homes where there is some real brokenness—alcoholism, drug addiction, abusive situations. You look at a person emerging from a family of origin with brokenness like that and they are, oftentimes, obsessed and in a frenzy to get married. They think that the other person can do what all the king's horses and all the king's men cannot do: "They can fix me. They can bandage me. They can heal me. They can make me whole."

Wrong.

Don't buy into the pipe-dream mentality that a certain special someone can fix everything. You are setting yourself up for some major disappointment if you believe that.

Inspecting for Cracks

I will never forget what happened when Lisa and I bought a home. We found a fourteen-year-old place and fell in love with it. Before we went to the mortgage company to put some money down and sign the stack of loan papers, we paid for an inspection. And since we were buying the house directly from the owner, we accompanied the inspector to the house.

When I walked in the front door, I saw the owners, the sellers, sitting on the hearth in the family room. I thought that was odd. I decided that they were being nice and giving us operating room to look around and see if everything was A-OK. I try to see the best in people. I'm a positive person.

The inspector looked around and saw a couple little things broken and messed up, but that was about it. We bought the house and were thrilled with our purchase. The day we moved in, I was helping the movers with some fireplace equipment and happened to put my foot on the hearth. To my shock the whole thing just split open. I don't want to name names, but, apparently, someone was covering up the crack in the mortar.

Dating, if you don't date very long, can be like hiding the cracks. It's not realistic. We put on our best clothes, our best cologne and perfume. We are on our best behavior with our best manners. We go to the best restaurants and the best movies. We always defer to one another, and we have that kind of mushy, puppy love for one another.

This is not the real world. Those first few months of dating are a fantasy world, an unrealistic la-la land of superficialities and misleading sensations. Both parties are sitting on cracked mortar, trying desperately to cover up fractures.

When people mistakenly think that this dating scenario is the real world, they end up marrying someone without really knowing that person. And then after two or three months or two or three years she realizes, "Wow, my spouse was sitting on some cracked mortar in his life before we got married. He is broken. He's messed up." If the couple had dated long enough to take a good look at the hearth, they might have seen the cracks before "buying the house."

Dealing with the Brokenness

When this realization comes (before or after marriage), when you begin to see pockets of brokenness, don't freak out. Don't say, "I'm out of here! I am bolting." None of us are perfect; we all have fractures and cracked mortar in our lives. If you take the time, though, to discover the brokenness while dating, you can call on a trusted Christian friend or a Christian counselor to process the brokenness before hooking up in marriage.

Don't have the Humpty Dumpty mentality and expect that your marriage partner is going to fix everything after you get married. Do the work now and move into marriage as two whole people who have already dealt with the shattered pieces of your past.

THE JACK 'N JILL TUMBLE

Here's another pre-nuptial nursery rhyme people often recite:

> Jack and Jill went up the hill to fetch a pail of water.
> Jack fell down and broke his crown and
> Jill came tumbling after.

A lot of Jack and Jillers say to themselves, "You know, if I get married, I will never, ever deal with isolation again. I will never, ever have a companionship yearning or be lonely again. For the rest of my life, I'll have someone to fetch pails of water with. Even if I fall and break my crown, I'll have someone to come tumbling after me. We are going to become just like Jack and Jill and that will be it. All of my companionship yearnings will be solved."

Filling the God Gap
To a degree, it is right to expect your spouse to fill

your companionship longings. But on another level, it is wrong. We have two basic levels of compatibility yearnings. The first one is the one I will call level A, and most of us are aware of this level. This level can be quenched, satisfied, through a deep friendship or a marriage. It is the yearning we have to be in community with another human being. We are wired for human relationships; God gives us this desire and that is a good thing.

However, there is a level B yearning that many of us don't realize is actually there. This is a God gap in our lives—a hole punctured in our hearts from birth that can only be filled through a personal connection with Jesus Christ.

A Recipe for Disappointment

Here is what happens. You put ingredient A—our human companionship yearnings—into the pot and add ingredient B—our God-gap companionship yearnings—into the pot. And you do the Julia Child thing and mix it up really well. Or maybe you do the Martha Stewart thing with the very expensive bowl and spoon. And when you have A and B converging, you suddenly have a double desire to get married. You think this human being can solve both level A and level B yearnings. Since you may not be aware of the level B yearnings or how to quench them, you put unrealistic expectations on the person you are marrying.

So one day you find yourselves in a church and the pastor is looking at you saying, "Having pledged your faith in and love to each other, having sealed your solemn and significant vows by the giving and receiving of these rings, acting by the authority given to me by the state of Texas and looking to heaven for divine sanction, I now pronounce you husband and wife in the presence of God and these assembled witnesses. What God has joined together, let no man separate."

The Jack and Jill nursery rhyme runs through your mind and you think to yourself, I will never deal with companionship yearnings again. Say what? Little does your new spouse know that, oftentimes, you are putting level B expectations on his or her shoulders. You are trying to get them to meet needs in your life that only God can meet. A human being can't fill the God gap. I can't do that for Lisa. She can't do that for me.

A *Futile Effort for Change*

When we become disappointed and disillusioned with our spouse's inability to meet our every need, we take our spouse and try to tweak them. We try to change them, mold them, and make them into what we think we need, inching them and nudging them into something they are not. That doesn't work, and we wake up one day with even more problems. Jack sees another Jill and he likes the way she walks up that hill and fetches her pail of water. He leaves, gets a divorce, and goes to this other person. Jill sees another Jack and goes down the hill after him.

The vicious cycle begins—divorce after divorce—until one day you look in the rear view mirror of life and see all of this relational wreckage. You have damaged your life, and maybe two or three other lives in the process. If there are children involved, you have messed them up too. Why? You didn't understand level B, the hole in your heart that only Christ can fill. Don't get caught in the Jack and Jill tumble. It is a fairy tale fallacy resulting in disappointment and failure.

THE MARITAL STREAM

Here's a pre-nuptial nursery rhyme that will, no doubt, sound very familiar to you:

Row, row, row your boat gently down the stream.
Merrily, merrily, merrily, merrily, life is but a dream.

But you may not have heard this rendition: "Row, row, row your boat gently down the marital stream. Merrily, merrily, merrily, merrily, marriage will be a dream." It's dreamy, all right. But you'd better be prepared for some bad dreams and an occasional nightmare.

Yet, I talk to people who tell me this, "When I get married, I will be complete and most of my problems will fade away. I am single and those problems are sticking to me now like Velcro™. But once I get married, no more of that junk. I'll live happily ever after. The white picket fence and 2.3 children."

It is so tempting to think this way. I know because I have said these rhymes before, too. Marriage is great. It is a wonderful thing. But a character transformation is not going to take place the moment you step over the line in holy matrimony. Ladies, if he is a jerk prior to marriage, he is going to be a world-class jerk after marriage. Hey guys, if she is a materialistic gold digger before marriage, she is going to be a major gold rush mama after marriage.

I CHALLENGE YOU TO LOOK FOR THOSE LITTLE RED FLAGS THAT ARE EVIDENT IN EVERY RELATIONSHIP, IF YOU'RE PAYING ATTENTION

I challenge you to look for those little red flags that are evident in every relationship, if you're paying attention. Those times when you think, "Oh, I don't like that," or, "That kind of gets on my nerves." Those little dislikes and discomforts will turn into monstrous flags billowing in the breeze when you are married.

The Single Advantage

The Apostle Paul addressed the single advantage in 1 Corinthians 7. Before we look at this text, let me set the context. Paul was writing these letters to the church at Corinth. We have a lot in common with this very metropolitan, worldly city of Corinth. Some of the people in the church at Corinth who were unmarried had some serious problems. They were worshipping idols and getting drunk at the communion table, among other things. So Paul told them that they need to think carefully about getting married and be aware of the special problems marriage might bring. They already had enough problems to deal with in their single lives, before adding the complexities and additional responsibilities of marriage.

That is why he wrote in 1 Corinthians 7:28, "But those who marry will face many troubles in this life...." The Living Bible says "extra problems." While most of us will get married at least once in our lifetime, God does give some individuals, a few of us, the gift of singleness. And it is a true gift. The text continues, "and I want to spare you this."

The Matrimonial Reality

Throughout this book, you will feel a tension, a cross-pull, and let me tell you why. On one hand, the single life is a viable, biblical lifestyle. It is a good thing if you are not married. On the other hand, being married is a viable, biblical lifestyle. It is also a good thing. But understand this right up front and read about it in God's word—marriage has problems.

Think about financial problems. He wants to buy a new set of golf clubs, and she wants a new sofa for the den. What about relational challenges? He wants to have his friends from college and their wives over, but she doesn't because all they talk about are sports. She wants to go out with some friends she met at church and their husbands, but he doesn't have anything in common with them.

And then there are the sexual problems. She was really feeling romantic last night, but he came in from work at 9:30. He is in the mood tonight, but she is tired and a little put out that he came home so late the night before. When the context of the relationship isn't right, she's not in the mood. He's often clueless about the context and doesn't understand why she's rebuffing his advances.

When you get married you have got to say, "I'm sorry," thousands of times. You have got to eat your words often and you have got to compromise, concede, and conciliate. And I haven't even touched on what happens when children come into the picture. But I think you are getting my point. I'm not trying to scare you away from marriage, but I want you to go into it—if you go into it—with eyes wide open.

Erasing the Scarlet Letter

It is time we take the word sin out of the word single. We think singles have this scarlet "S" on them. One of the major problems that I see with the evangelical churches across our country is that they cringe at the word "Single!" But let's look at some biblical trivia. A lot of prophets in the Old Testament were what? Single. The Apostle Paul was...single. Jesus Christ, you know this one, was...single. Yet most churches today would reject these biblical personalities I just mentioned simply because they are single. Where did we go wrong?

At Fellowship Church we do not frown on hiring staff who are single. On the contrary, we believe that singles have a unique perspective, commitment, and dedication to ministry that many who are married are unable to have. Don't discount your single days or waste them away until you get married. If you do, you'll be blowing the incredible opportunities for ministry you can have before the unique problems and responsibilities of marriage set in.

From Nursery Rhymes to Biblical Reason

Learn the 4:12 Secret

If you are doing the Hickory Dickory Dock dance, here is your challenge. Learn the secret of Philippians 4:12, "I have learned the secret of being content in any and every situation, whether well fed or hungry, whether living in plenty or in want." And remember verse 13 also, "I can do everything through him who gives me strength."

Contentment is the tranquility of your soul, satisfaction with where you are and confidence in God for your future. Let me tell you something from experience. If you are not content as a single, you are not going to gain contentment the moment you get married. A relational rock on the ring finger of your left hand is not going to get you there.

This, though, is what the evil one wants you to do. The evil one wants you to so concentrate on what you do not have—I don't have my man...I don't have my girl...I don't have my dream home—that you miss your single shot and all the unique opportunities it can bring right now. You miss this incredible season when you can be scoring touchdowns, shooting three pointers, and knocking the ball out of the park for the glory of God. Incorporate the 4:12 secret into your life now, while you are single, and it will continue to serve you well when you are married.

Discover The Real Fix

Hey, Humpty Dumpter, you know who you are. Here is a word of advice for you from Psalm 147:3, "He heals the brokenhearted." "He" is not a spouse. Only God can do that kind of repair work. Only He can fix your fracture and bind up your wounds. Allow the great physician to bandage you up, to heal you, to fix you. Don't sit on that hearth and try to cover up the cracks in the mortar, hoping your potential mate won't notice.

Give Peace a Chance

If you're playing Jack and Jill on the hill, here is what you need to do. Give peace a chance. I am not talking about some LSD-driven, John Lennon, Yoko Ono, Hari

Krishna-type trip. I am talking about the peace that surpasses all understanding, peace that only comes through a personal relationship with Christ. John 14:27 says,

> Peace I leave with you; [it doesn't come from a spouse]
> my peace I give you. I do not give to you as the world gives.
> Do not let your hearts be troubled and do not be afraid.

Join the Advantage Club

If you are row, row, rowing your boat up that marital stream, thinking that marriage is a dream, join the Advantage Club—the Single Advantage. Look again at 1 Corinthians 7, verses 32-34,

> I would like you to be free from concern. An unmarried man [this includes unmarried women] is concerned about the Lord's affairs, how he can please the Lord. But a married man is concerned about the affairs of this world, how he can please his wife, and his interests are divided.

Do you know what really fires me up? I get excited when I think about all of the singles who are involved in the ministries of Fellowship Church. These people commit to three, maybe four, ministries because they have time. They are taking their single shots and taking advantage of this season of their lives. They are shooting three pointers, scoring touchdowns, knocking the ball out of the park for the glory of God. Our church is made up of almost 50 percent singles and we couldn't survive without them. And your church can't survive without singles either.

Also, if you are single and part of this Advantage Club, think about the friendship factor. You can have more and deeper relationships with others. You can have many more deep friendships than I can, because I am married and have four children. My time, energies, and priorities are more divided. You have a single shot in the Advantage Club. Enjoy it while you can.

IN THE MIDST OF MINISTRY

I was talking to my brother awhile back about his ministry with single adults. At the time, Ben was running one of the largest church single's ministries in America. He is also a noted author and for many years was the only Christian singles-driven talk show host in the country. I'm going to give a shameless plug for his books, *The 10 Commandments of Dating* and *The One*. Check them out. They are well worth the read.

He asked me, "Ed, do you know what the single biggest problem is that I deal with in my ministry to single adults?"

I said, "What? Materialism? Pre-marital sex?"

He responded, "No, none of those things. It is single adults who jump from church to church. It is church hopping, never plugging into the life and ministry of a local church."

Many singles are always looking for the hottest scene. "Oh, this church over here has it going on. I had better hang out here for awhile." "Wow! Look at the babes over there. I like that Jill. I like that Jack." Then they get tired of that, they've dated everyone they want to there, so they go to another church and check it out.

What is so thrilling about Fellowship Church is that we have a core group of singles that are life-timers. They are engaged and involved, with roots that run deep into the life and ministry of the church.

Now, I am partial to Fellowship, but there are many great churches around. Don't float. Don't hop and bop. There is no such thing as a Christian floater in the Bible. Get hooked up to a local church, because it is in the midst of your involvement in the church—learning the secret of contentment, discovering the real fix, giving peace a chance, and joining the Advantage Club—that you are likely to find the kind of person God wants for you as a covenant partner.

CHAPTER
2

THE ULTI-MATE RIDE
Fixing the Flaws of Defective Dating

It happens in the automotive industry with a striking regularity. Cars, trucks, vans, even SUVs are recalled because of defective parts. A few years ago it happened to me. I received this letter from the Ford Motor Company:

> Dear Mr. Young,
>
> This notice is sent to you in accordance with the requirements of the National Traffic and Motor Vehicles Safety Act. Ford Motor Company has decided that certain 1999 super-duty F250 and F350 trucks failed to conform to Federal motor vehicle safety standard no. 301. During fuel system integrity testing, fuel may leak at a higher rate than allowed by regulation. Call your dealer without delay. Ask for a service date and whether parts are in stock for safety recall 99F11.

When I received this letter, I didn't ignore it. I got the problem fixed. A thinking person wouldn't even entertain the thought of ignoring a recall letter.

I want to address in this book something in many people's lives that is defective—something that needs to be recalled. It is not an automobile. It is something much more important than that. I'm talking about dating. Most of the dating that is done today is defective. Think about it. Would you drive a defective car? Would you tool around in a car that has a part that could endanger your life and the lives of others? Of course, your answer is, "No, that would be reckless and stupid." Yet, far too many of us date in a defective way, endangering our lives and the lives of others.

The majority of spouse selection going on today is skewed and needs to be recalled. You might be thinking at this point, "Ed, what a broad-brushed and generalized statement. Come on. You're telling me that more people than not are defective daters?" Yes, it doesn't take a social scientist or relational guru to see that we are messing up. If you don't believe me, consider the following statistics:

- *The US has the highest divorce rate in the world as a percentage of population*

- *Out of every ten marriages that take place in the US, five will end in divorce[1]*

- *The average length of all marriages in the US is 9.8 years[2]*

- *One out of every three children born in the US is born to an unwed woman*

- *One out of every four children in the US lives with a single parent[3]*

Even children are seeing that the way we are currently doing spouse selection is not working. One evening when my son E.J. was about eight, my family and I were seated around our kitchen table having dinner. E.J. said, "Mom, Dad, a friend of mine told me today that his parents are getting a divorce."

We said, "Oh, E.J., we're sorry. Show your friend a little extra care; be sensitive to him."

Then one of our twin daughters said, "Mommy, Daddy, will you guys ever get a divorce?"

Lisa reassured her, "No, we won't."

The twin responded by saying, "Thank you. Thank you."

This issue of dating and spouse selection is important for everyone, because it impacts society at so many different levels. Maybe you have recently gone

THIS ISSUE OF DATING AND SPOUSE SELECTION IS IMPORTANT FOR EVERYONE, BECAUSE IT IMPACTS SOCIETY AT SO MANY DIFFERENT LEVELS.

through a divorce and you are just stepping back into the dating scene. Maybe you are a twenty-something, or thirty-something, or forty-something single adult and you have never been married. Maybe you are a single parent. Maybe you are a student. Even if you are currently married and a parent, you need to pay attention to this issue, because the moment our children are born we are involved in an intense spouse selection process. Whether we know it or not, we are mirroring to them how to choose their mate.

Throughout the remainder of this chapter and the next, I want to bring to light some flaws of defective dating. And, hopefully, the exposure of these flaws will teach us what to do by making clear what not to do. To illustrate the various problems I am going to pinpoint, I want you to picture in your mind a Mercedes Benz convertible. That's right, a brand new, top of the line, pop top Benz.

The Mercedes 500SL convertible is a dream car for a lot of people. Almost no one, really, would turn down a ride in this fine automobile. And I want you to keep a picture of the ultimate ride in your mind's eye as we discuss God's ultimate in dating and selecting a mate. I call it finding your "ulti-mate."

STEERING DEFICIT DISORDER

The first flaw of defective dating is that people don't take enough time to see who's behind the wheel—the person who is driving the relationship. If you don't see who is behind the wheel, you have a great chance of messing up on one of the most important decisions you'll ever make—choosing the person you will marry.

Do you know what the Bible says? The Bible says that the person behind the wheel has towering implications on the relationship, in dating, in marriage, and later in the challenges of child rearing. The Scriptures tell us that Christ-followers should only date and marry other Christians, true believers. In other words, we should make sure that Jesus Christ has the keys.

Well, how do you do that? How do you know that your date or potential mate is a true believer? A true believer always has a "How I gave Christ the keys" story. And they should be able and willing to share with you what kind of driving Christ has been doing in their life since the key transfer. If someone does not have that story, they are not a believer. They are not a Christ-follower. Even if they have known about Christ since they were a child, they should still be able to articulate how they gave their life to Christ and what that means to them now.

If someone only says, "I've always been a Christian," watch out. If someone says, "My parents were Christians and I grew up in church," watch out. These statements do not reflect a personal decision of giving one's self to Christ, of transferring the keys to Him.

This is the most fatal flaw that I see on the dating scene among Christians today. Too many are compromising their most fundamental beliefs by getting intimately involved with non-believers. I cannot stress strongly enough that you are inviting disaster when you do this. You may not see the storm clouds right away, but watch the horizon. The storms will come and they will be devastating.

The Bible shares with us a highly unpopular text in 2 Corinthians 6:14, "Do not be yoked together with unbelievers. For what do righteousness and wickedness have in common? Or what fellowship can light have with darkness?"

When singles read this text you would think they would say, "Okay, God is the creator of marriage and surely He knows the best way to select a spouse. I am going to do it God's way." Instead most singles shake their heads because this verse eliminates a large amount of potential prospects. And many singles, when they read this, say, "Wait a minute! It is hard enough to find someone who is sane and healthy. Now they have to be a believer, too? That's pretty heavy."

Some see this word yoke and they say, "Yoke, what a joke. Aren't egg yokes supposed to be bad for you anyway? I am an egg-white guy. I am an egg-white girl."

Yoke is an agriculture term that we need to grasp the meaning of, if we hope to be hooked up with the right guy or girl in marriage. A yoke is simply a wooden contraption that goes around the neck of animals and is tethered to a plow. When animals were equally yoked, for example, oxen of equal strength, then the farmer could plow the fields in straight lines. If he had one animal that was stronger than the other, the yoke and the plow and the farmer would be pulling against each other. They would be pulled off course. This whole process would be direction less.

If we want to have a great marriage, we have got to be equally connected. Jesus Christ must be driving the vehicle. He must be driving our vehicle and the vehicle of the person we are considering hooking up with. Don't date nonbelievers because you can fall in love with a nonbeliever. And, if you do, you will never reach your full potential.

At this point, some defective daters begin to tell rational lies to themselves. They say, "Oh, I am going to take my unbelieving hottie, and I am going to win him to the Lord. He will say a little prayer and get a little baptized, be a part of the little church and everything will cruise. This freeway is going to be so smooth...."

Singles, let me tell you something. In the heat of a dating relationship, the other person will do anything, say anything, get baptized any way just to be with you. You cannot trust a hormone-driven decision while you are dating this person. If you are dating someone and this someone is not a believer, back off. Don't date him. Don't date her. Then watch and see what happens. If they become a Christ-follower, if they grow and Jesus becomes fully formed in their life over the next year or two or three, then think about dating. But not any time before that.

God Knows Your Ulti-Mate Destination

I am a why person, always asking, "Why?" Why would God set forth these standards? Is God being restrictive? No. God is being protective, and He wants the best for you and the best for me. That is why I picked a Mercedes 500SL, a $90,000 sports car, as an illustration. This is one of the best cars made. But in God's economy, your life and mine makes this incredible car look like a wreck. That's how much we are loved and the kind of potential we have.

God wants to spare us the pain and agony of being unequally yoked, of being hooked up with another human being who does not have the same strength or the same octane or the same RPMs that Christ brings. Why? God wants us to be equally yoked with believers because His desire for us is that we reach our ulti-mate destination.

That is what dating is all about—to find the ulti-mate. I don't care how casual it is. I don't care how flippant it is. Down deep, I'm talking even to guys now. You are thinking, "Could she be the one? Could she be my wife, the mother of my children? Could I grow old with her?" And I know, women, that you are thinking the same kinds of thoughts about the men you date.

Do you want to reach your ulti-mate destination? Do you want to hit on all eight cylinders? Then connect with another Christ-follower. Frankly, my heart is grieved and broken for so many people who make the wrong call, thinking they can somehow reach their ulti-mate destination without being equally yoked. It is a formula for failure.

God Has the Owner's Manual

Another reason why God insists on us being equally

yoked is that He wants you and me to read from the same owner's manual. The Benz has an owner's manual, and part of the owner's manual deals with troubleshooting issues. I have heard rumors that, in marriage, conflict can occur. Some arguments can happen from time to time. And here's why. The marital math is pretty basic. One sinner plus another sinner equals double trouble. But the moment I receive Christ into my life, He gives me the ministry of reconciliation through the power of His Spirit and His owner's manual—the Bible.

That means when I do something wrong against my lovely wife Lisa, the Holy Spirit begins to work on me and remind me of what God says in His owner's manual. He nudges me and says, "Ed, Jesus died on the cross for you and rose again. You don't deserve it, but He did it. And He forgives you and took the initiative to reconcile you to God. Do the same to your wife." When those marital troubles hit, we both have the ministry of reconciliation, and we reconcile.

If you hook up with someone who is not using the same owner's manual as you, you are in serious trouble. It is just a matter of time before your marriage is broken and banged up and becomes wreckage on the relational road.

God Charted the Parent Map

Another reason why God insists on this compatibility issue is that He wants us to study the same parent map. Most of us, when we get married, will have children. Child rearing is, bar none, the most challenging responsibility you will ever take on. My wife and I have four children, and parenthood is both the most difficult and rewarding thing we've ever done. But, as difficult as it is, it would be impossible if we were not on the same page in our parenting agenda.

I cannot even imagine what it would be like to try to parent without a unified front. I couldn't even entertain the thought of parenting my children with Lisa driving one way and me going another way. That's why we read and study the same parent map. We have similar values, transcendent truths given to us from God, which we teach together to our children. And those values and beliefs are reinforced by making the church central to our family life.

Don't you see the genius of God? He is not being restrictive; He is being protective. He wants the best for you and the

DON'T YOU SEE THE GENIUS OF GOD? HE IS NOT BEING RESTRICTIVE; HE IS BEING PROTECTIVE. HE WANTS THE BEST FOR YOU AND THE BEST FOR ME.

best for me. Too many of us, though, are caught up in superficial distractions and never look at the most important thing. Is the person you are dating, considering as a mate, truly a Christ-follower?

THE SHOWROOM MENTALITY

Another flaw of defective dating is what I call the showroom mentality. Talk to car dealers and they will tell you about the twenty-four hour principle. They will tell you that when American men and women think about buying a car, walk into the showroom, look at the lines, and focus on a few features of the car, most of them will drive away with the car in the first twenty-four to forty-eight hours. They make a quick decision based on just a few features. That is the showroom mentality.

How many American men and women focus on just a couple of superficial features without thinking about the whole car? How many people consider marriage without reading the maintenance record, the warranty, Consumer Reports? How many make the second most important choice of their life, aside from their relationship with Christ, based on incomplete and faulty facts?

Marital statistics bear out that too many of us have and continue to make these mistakes. I could tell you about many sad situations of people who have this showroom mentality. Romance is important. Feeling that feeling is important. But your relationship cannot be built on romance. And one day your children will ask you this question, "How do I know if he or she is the one?" And most of the time parents just smile and answer, "You will just know."

No! That is not good enough. You just know? Are we going to buy into this Hollywood-style, quiver-in-your-liver definition of love? "I have got to have that 'loving feeling.' And when I feel that, it's going to be a slam-dunk, a no-brainer. It's going to be love at first sight." It doesn't work that way.

Fleeting Love

There are two types of love. Eros is that erotic, obsessive, mysterious aspect of love. It has got to be there. God has given us the chemistry, the desire for the opposite sex. That is a good thing. Your potential spouse should be someone you are attracted to. Your heart should beat fast when you see this person. But I will tell you one more time. A relationship cannot be built on eros alone, because eros usually only lasts nine months to a year.

I remember the first year in my relationship with Lisa. It was eros-driven, romance-driven. I wanted to be with her every second of every day. But I dated her long enough to let the eros—the passionate romantic love—fall into its proper place. Romance has to be ruled within the context of the total relationship. Too many times we focus on a few features. We feel that romance stuff going on, and we take off down the aisle. Push the clock forward three years—we wake up one Saturday morning, the eros has faded, and we look at our spouse and wonder, "Who are you?"

Lasting Love

There is another kind of love. Agape love is that commitment-based love. It is that nurturing and companionship love. Any great relationship must be built on agape and, when it is, when that is the foundation, eros love will ebb and flow. Lisa and I have built our marriage on agape and it has gotten stronger and stronger. Because of that foundation of lasting love, the eros part has also grown and flourished. But, too often, students, single parents, those who are playing the dating game, those who have been recently divorced, get duped into thinking that "feeling it" will mean they have found "the one."

One of my favorite verses of Scripture is 1 Samuel 16:7.

Here is what God told Samuel. "The Lord does not look at the things man looks at. Man looks at the outward appearance but the Lord looks at the heart." We need to do the same thing. The passion must be there but it is a heart issue, not a couple of outward, superficial features. Are you a defective dater who needs to pay attention to the recall notice and say, "You know what? I've been involved in this showroom floor mentality. I need to change."

OFF-ROAD HAZARDS

A third flaw of defective dating involves the off-road hazards of sexuality. You will not hear this talked about in the church very much. The church has messed up royally on this one, because it has not articulated clearly enough over the years the biblical stance regarding premarital sex. Chapter four will go into greater detail on this, but I must take some time to address it here as one of the most serious dating hazards.

What if I just took the keys to a Mercedes 500SL and gave them to you. What if I said, "You are a great girl or guy. I want to give you this $90,000, eight cylinder Mercedes convertible. Here you go." You know what you would say? "Man, Ed is my favorite person. I just love that guy." And I will tell you what you would also do. If you received those keys, you would take care of the car. You would garage it. You would wash it. You would park it by itself to keep it from getting door dings. And you would drive this very expensive car where it is supposed to be driven—on the road. You would not take it off-road.

Yet, too many times we take this gift of sex given to us by God—this Mercedes Benz, this desire that is to be practiced on God's freeway, on His Autobahn, between His guardrails—and use it in a God-forbidden way. We jump in the back seat, we put a ramp right next to God's guardrail, rev up the engines like Robby Knievel, and we go off-road. This car has been built, tested, and approved for city and highway travel. It does not have four-wheel drive and is not meant for joyriding through field and stream. Mud would get all over the place and cloud your vision. The car would get stuck and the more you pressed the accelerator, the deeper it would go.

That's what happens when we do sex our way instead of God's way.

"Oh, yeah. Right, God. You created sex. You are pro-sex. You have told me five times directly and twenty-three times indirectly to abstain from sex until marriage. But you know, God, I know more than You know about this. I am just going to go off-road, because I would rather experience the thrills and chills of sex than do what I should be doing in dating—building communication, working through conflict resolution, and understanding whether or not we are spiritually and emotionally compatible."

This off-road mentality is why so many people marry the wrong person and, as a result, so many marriages fail. It is the power of sex. Sex blinds us and then it *binds* us. It is a multi-faceted practice, impacting us physically, spiritually, psychologically, and emotionally. Mud gets all over us and the more we get involved, the more we press the accelerator, the deeper we go. We look over at this person, and we can't tell if he or she is right for us or not. And we fall in lust, not in love, and marry them.

Recognizing the Biblical Guardrails

Paul wrote something regarding sexuality to a group of people in the first century with whom, I believe, we can identify today. The Thessalonians lived in a very sexually-saturated culture. Extramarital sex was applauded. In some of the Greek religions of their day it was called an act of worship, believe it or not. And don't think we have one up on them, that they were barbarians and we are somehow above that kind of depravity.

All you have to do is channel surf, surf the net, or

just live life to see the bombardment of degrading sexual images and ideas that permeate our culture. The world does a God-ordained thing in a God-forbidden way. But, obviously, the world's way is not working.

In 1 Thessalonians 4:3–5 Paul tells the Thessalonian church,

> It is God's will that you should be sanctified [the word sanctified simply means more dedicated to God]: that you should avoid sexual immorality; that each of you should learn to control his own body in a way that is holy and honorable, not in passionate lust like the heathen, who do not know God.

The Bible gives several biblical boundaries regarding sex. The first word the Bible uses is *adultery*. Adultery is what happens when someone who is married engages in sexual activity with someone other than his or her spouse. The next word is *fornication*. Fornication means having sex before marriage. The third concept is *sexual immorality*. That a general term which includes heavy physical contact up to the point of sexual intercourse.

You may have thought, as do many others, "I cannot have sexual intercourse until I get married, but I guess God gives me the green light to do everything else up until that point." I hate to rain on your sexual party, but God's design for sex relates to more than just actual sexual intercourse. There are basically three gears that pastors, theologians, and counselors have pinpointed regarding a physical relationship with someone prior to marriage.

The first gear is the kissing and the hugging stage. The second gear is the caressing stage, or sensual contact with your clothes on. The third gear is the stimulation stage, genital contact that often leads to climax. Sexual immorality occurs when you go into the second and third gear.

This heavy sexual activity just short of intercourse can cause guilt, separation, and alienation in the relationship. You are committing sexual immorality when you do those things, and you are damaging your relationship. God's plan—God's standard—for sex is designed to bring unity and closeness in the relationship, not alienation and guilt. Only within the context of a committed marriage before God can we truly experience all aspects of sex in the way God intended.

On the Road Again

Well, you may say, "Ed, I have messed up sexually. My virginity is past tense." Or maybe you are "technically" a virgin but have lived in third gear for a long time. "You mean, Ed, that I should stop at first gear? I am sexually experienced. I can't stop." Oh, yes you can.

I have a close friend in Houston who was very promiscuous before he became a Christ follower. Then he gave his life and his sexuality to the Lord. A few years later he met a beautiful young woman, and he stayed in first gear for a year until his wedding night. And he will tell you that God did great things for him in that area of his life. He shared with me a few years ago, "Ed, I have been with a lot of women. I know that God has forgiven it and forgotten it, but I wish I had saved myself for my spouse."

If you haven't lost your virginity, don't. Give your spouse the ultimate gift on your wedding night. If you have, God will forgive you. He will cleanse you. He can remake you and remold you. So stop having sex until you get married and God will truly bless that area in your life. Don't you see, again, that God wants the best for us? He doesn't want us to trash His gift. He doesn't want us to go off-road. He doesn't want us to make a poor decision based on the power of sex.

Maybe you are thinking, "You know, Ed, this whole defective dating deal is a picture of me. Talk about not looking behind the wheel, that's me. Talk about showroom mentality, that's me. Talk about going off-road, that's me." Come to the Lord and He will fix the flaw.

He can change a defective part, if you'll just pay attention to the recall notification.

In the next chapter, we'll look at one more major flaw of defective dating. Defective daters will look at the car and check it out, but they fail to pop the trunk. Who can blame them? It's hard to look at what's in the trunk, the baggage that all of us carry. This baggage blunder is a big one and actually leads to three other dating flaws.

CHAPTER
3

∞∞

CHECKS AND BALANCES
*Reading and Heeding the Warning Signs
in a Relationship*

In this chapter, we're going to look at four more flaws of defective dating. All of these involve, to one extent or another, checks and balances in the relationship that are often neglected or ignored. If you're paying attention to the warning signs—the road signs, the red flags, the cargo in the trunk—you're in good shape. This means you are engaged in the relationship with your eyes wide open and your radar at full scan.

Sadly, though, many people date and enter serious relationships wearing side-blinders. They get caught up in the superficial aspects of dating and are simply not paying attention to the deeper, lasting issues that need to be examined in a long-term commitment. God wants you to use your common sense and good judgment when considering a commitment like marriage, and you've got to clue into the checks and balances He provides along the way in order to truly find your ulti-mate.

Bags 'N Baggage

Defective daters will look at the car and check it out, but they fail to pop the trunk and examine the luggage. Who can blame them? It's hard to look at the emotional, spiritual, and relational baggage that all of us carry. This baggage blunder can lead to all sorts of other problems and, in particular, we'll look at three other dating flaws that stem from baggage neglect.

Ladies, I know your hottie seems so perfect right now, so unbelievable, but in reality he is Samsonite Sam—loaded down with suitcases. Guys, I know that babe you have your eye on, that girl that you have been dating, looks like the ulti-mate. She could be the one, but she is also Louis Vuitton Linda—weighted down with a bunch of baggage.

Before you say "I do," you'd better look at the junk in the trunk, on the luggage rack, and inside the loaded-down U-Haul trailer that some people pull behind them.

Let me reiterate, once again, that we all are loaded

down with luggage. Baggage doesn't really cause problems unless we pretend like we don't have it or unless we are unwilling to process it. The blunder comes not from the existence of baggage but from ignorance and neglect in dealing with it.

The Family Duffel

The first bag is called the family duffel. People who do spouse selection God's way will really check out the family situation. Why? Because the family dynamic wields the most power. It has the most influence on who you are and who I am. That is where our self-esteem was formed and our value system was learned. We, for the most part, understood what marriage is all about from our upbringing.

The family formula is major, so make sure you take some time out of your busy dating schedules to open the family duffel and look through the contents. You must have intentional conversations related to your family's high points and low points.

The family bag is important to inspect because it is often the cause of a lot of dings and scratches and dents in our lives. No one comes from his or her original family unscathed. No one emerges from imperfect parents looking like a brand new Mercedes Benz. Even those

THE FAMILY BAG IS IMPORTANT TO INSPECT BECAUSE IT IS OFTEN THE CAUSE OF A LOT OF DINGS AND SCRATCHES AND DENTS IN OUR LIVES.

coming from the best of families are still banged and bruised a little bit. Your parents were not perfect. My parents were not perfect. And our parent's parents weren't perfect either.

So many in today's society grow up into Blaming Boomers or Generation Excusers, who love to say that they are the way they are because their mother put their diapers on too tight or the nursery was painted the wrong color. They blame, whine, and claim that they are the victims. For the most part our parents did the best they could at that time, and it's time to take responsibility for ourselves and say: "You know what? This is my family. I am who I am. It is time to deal with the baggage." So make sure you talk about it.

Romans 3:10 is a great baggage verse. It says, "There is no one righteous, not even one." In other words, we all have baggage called sin. Sin is imperfection or missing God's mark. Sin loads every individual and family down and causes lots of cargo carnage. The key is how we deal with the carnage in our lives, both past and present. Ignoring it is not the solution.

Wise spouse selectors open the trunk and carefully inspect the family bag. They also make their own family duffel available for a thorough search. Like an airport security agent searching a bag, you need to keep your eyes open for potential problems and then deal openly and honestly with them—before you get married, not after.

The Temperament Carry-on

Spouse selectors also need to open another bag—the temperament carry-on. Each of us is wired in a unique way, just like different machines are wired in unique ways. For example, the Mercedes 500SL is wired much differently than a Ford F250 pickup truck. Because you are wired differently than the person you are dating, you had better talk about the wiring challenges. Maybe you are a planner and you have got to have everything organized just so. You can't function without your Palm Pilot or Day-Timer at your fingertips. On the other hand, the person that you have your eye on is a spontaneous, off-the-cuff individual who likes to make it up as they go. They like to get behind the wheel, take a left turn, or maybe go straight as the mood strikes them. They might even enjoy an unplanned day trip, but you prefer an ultra-planned weekend excursion. This is a wiring challenge that must be addressed.

Maybe you are a spender who likes go to the mall and shop till you drop. You like to take financial risk with investments, but the other person is much more conservative, playing it close to the vest. You have got to think about and talk about this difference.

The temperament challenges are those day-to-day irritations that cause friction and create tension in marriage. Out of the blue the wife will look at her husband and say, "The way you chew ice drives me nuts." The husband will look at the wife and say, "The way you organize your shoes, honey, please, I can't take it anymore."

Conflicting Styles

You can't say the word temperament without saying the word "temper." This leads to the major issue of how we handle conflict, which is directly related to how our family of origin handled conflict. How did your mother or father, or your potential mate's parents, deal with car trouble, wrecks, problems along life's journey?

Maybe you grew up in a family that handled conflict SWAT style, where the hurt party just started firing verbal shots at everyone else. You might have grown up in a family that handled conflict frappuccino style, where the standard response was to ice the other person out. Or perhaps your family handled conflict ziplock style, collecting the negative pain and anguish, cramming it into a Ziplock bag and placing it in the refrigerator. It sits there for two or three months, until someone opens the refrigerator one day and POW!

I want to save you a lot of time and trouble about conflict resolution. I have been married for twenty years and have gone through a number of different disagreements and arguments. I have boiled it down to this—almost all conflict is over PMS. Don't get mad at me. I am not referring to the PMS you are thinking about, ladies. I am talking about P, power issues. In the process of becoming "one flesh," the "I" fights for survival and neither person wants to give up personal control. M stands for money. Statistics bear out time and again that most of the marital mayhem we deal with is over finances. And then there is the big S, representing sexual issues. It is tough enough just to remain sexually pure until you get married, to stay on God's autobahn and not go off-road. Bet even after marriage, you will have sexual compatibility disagreements.

Well, the Bible has an answer for all conflicts both prior to and within marriage, no matter what particular issues they stem from. God tells us in Ephesians 4:15 to speak the truth in love. Proverbs 15:1 says, "A gentle answer turns away wrath, but a harsh word stirs up anger." The Bible also says in Ephesians 4:26 that we should not let the sun set on our anger. You can count on one thing in any relationship—you are going to have conflict.

Whether it's a power issue, a money issue, or a sexual issue, how you deal with conflict will be the saving grace in your dating relationship and in your marriage. Take time to find out about your potential mate's family conflict style and temperament, and then begin to discover together how God's guidelines and boundaries for conflict can bring healing, reconciliation, and greater intimacy in your relationship.

DASHBOARD WARNINGS

Something else that defective daters do is to ignore the dashboard warning lights and gauges. Maybe you have seen the dashboard of a Mercedes, which resembles the cockpit of a 747. I am continually amazed by all of the dashboard warning lights, buzzers, and voices that communicate with us in the computerized vehicles we drive today. Sometimes these technological bells and whistles get on our nerves, but they are designed to warn us and protect us.

One day I was tooling around in my truck and I noticed that the fuel gauge had been on full for the last three days. At the time I was driving a Ford F250, 4 x 4, that drinks fuel so fast I can almost watch the fuel gauge go down while I'm driving. I knew the gas tank could not still be full, so I decided that it was broken and I probably needed gas. I pulled into a service station and put in $41 worth of fuel. For three days I was just into the trip, not really paying attention to my fuel gauge, until it was almost too late. If I hadn't realized at the last minute that the gauge was stuck, I would have ended up stranded on the side of the road.

Many of us date in much the same way. We're not paying attention to the dashboard warnings, because we are just into the trip. "Oh, forget the warning lights. I don't need any gauges to tell me what to do." There are several warning lights, gauges, and signals that you need to monitor in any serious relationship. Ignoring them is a recipe for disaster.

The Character Gauge

First of all, you need to monitor the character gauge of the person you are dating. I can't say this very often, but the political jargon of recent campaigns is right—it is all about character. Is this person responsible? Does this person have a high personal integrity value? Does this person have a consistency and a predictability in their personality and habits?

Some say, "Well, you know, he just has a little gambling problem." This is a character problem. Are you watching the gauge? These "little problems" have a tendency to get bigger, blow up, and cause relational wrecks once you get married. "Well, she has a little drinking and drug problem. It's really not that bad." Who are you trying to kid?

Ask yourself this question—Can I hang out with this person as my spouse for the next 20, 30, 40, 50 years and respect their character? Or how about this question—Do I want to have the same character that they have? These are tough questions that must be asked if you're serious about having a life-long, Christ-honoring relationship.

The Relational Rearview Mirror

Another indicator to look at is the relational rearview mirror. When you are trying to find the ulti-mate, you had better look at how they have handled relationships, past and present. Look in the rearview mirror of their lives and assess the relational history. Does he or she have long-term, nurturing friendships? Is he or she pretty square with their parents. Do they have a good reputation on the dating scene or have they left a string of relational wreckage behind them?

If everything looks good, then that's great. But if it doesn't look good, if they have a short track record with relationships or problems with their parents, always bickering and arguing, you'd better pay attention.

The Maintenance Light

The next warning sign is the maintenance light, or, more appropriately, the high maintenance light. This one is costly, because it requires frequent tune-ups and service calls. If you look on your dashboard and see dollar signs flashing, if you pick up vibes about the other person's need to drive a certain car, live in a certain zip code, or wear only certain clothes, listen carefully to the following advice.

Here is what you need to do—get out of the car, go to another dealership, and try out another car. You need to understand the BMW or Bangladesh theory. The person you marry must be equally satisfied if you are driving seventeen BMWs or if God leads you to a mission opportunity in Bangladesh feeding the hungry. If they aren't, head for the hills.

When I think about Lisa, I am so glad I dated her long enough to see these issues play out. Lisa is a woman with an impeccable character, high integrity and morals. One of the reasons I married her is because she is so consistent. I never wonder how she will act, how she will process dealing with a family that is really poor or another family that has millions of dollars. I never wonder if she will be swayed by any of that. She never is.

I think about her relationships. I look back in her life and see people who love her and honor her, and I can see how Christ-centered her relationships are. Lisa is also low maintenance. She has never insisted on living in a certain house or neighborhood, driving a certain car, or wearing a certain label on her clothes. This speaks volumes about who she is as a person and how she relates to me as a husband.

Now, I am not saying that Lisa and I are perfect. We are just like you—fellow strugglers. But I am saying to you, and this is so important, that you have got to be very intentional about seeing and processing these dashboard warnings. And you have got to date long enough to really be able to see them with any clarity and honesty.

Love is not blind, only temporarily impaired during the infatuation stage of the relationship. When the blinders of initial infatuation are taken off, these various warning signs will begin to hit you. And it is a far preferable scenario for them to

> **LOVE IS NOT BLIND, ONLY TEMPORARILY IMPAIRED DURING THE INFATUATION STAGE OF THE RELATIONSHIP.**

appear before you are married than after. Also, don't ignore your family, your friends or others in your life who see warning signs that you are apt to miss. They have an objective perspective that you can't possibly have in the midst of the relationship.

THE TEST-DRIVE DECEPTION

Another defective dating habit involves taking this car illustration too far. The rationale of those who engage in this flaw goes something like this, "I'll take a test-drive before I get married. Come on, I wouldn't walk into a dealer, plunk down $90,000 and take a Mercedes home without at least going through a test-drive. So I think I should at least take my potential mate out for a little spin." This is a common rationale these days in dating. "I'll just cohabitate with the person, play a little house and try things out for a while before I seal the deal."

The logic sounds so good, and I understand why people would buy into it. Because so many adults are the products of broken homes, they don't want to go through that wreckage again with the person they marry. Some also say they do it for financial reasons or to see if the love is real.

Sex, No Pink Slip Required

People today are living together prior to marriage in record numbers, and let me tell you why I believe that's happening. Let's start with the reason men do it. Do you know why, ladies, guys are living with you? Two words: free sex. It is the best of both worlds for guys. They can glean the sexual benefits of marriage without the commitment. Do you remember in the movie Grease how guys would drag race for the pink slip, the certificate of title, of their opponent? Well, guys today are living with women so that they can have the sex without the legality, the official union, of marriage. Now some ladies might say, "Ed, you don't know my man. You don't know the man I am test-driving. Surely he is not living with me just for sex."

Well, if you don't believe me, let me give you some homework. Go to the apartment or house where you are doing the test drive, sit down at the kitchen table, look into his eyes and say this, "Baby, for the next two months we are not having sex." He'll be out of there in a couple of weeks. Ladies, men won't tell you this, but I want to save you some pain.

Marital Manipulation

Now, ladies, do you know why you test-drive? It is not

because of sex. I know ladies enjoy that, but that's not it for them. It is because you think you can manipulate your man into marriage. Research reveals that over 70 percent of women who test-drive, who cohabitate, have marriage on their mind. And the remaining percent are living in denial.

A survey done by The Houston Chronicle reported that women who lived with their man before marriage had an 80 percent higher chance of divorce than those ladies who did not live with their man. Washington State University did another study, revealing that ladies who test drive with their boyfriends are twice as likely to battle depression and encounter domestic violence than those who do not.

Hit the Brakes

If you are test-driving, let me give you a pastoral word. Do it God's way. Put the brakes on and move out to different residences. You can still date the person, but you have to wait for the sexual part until marriage. I would challenge you to let many, many months go by until you know you have saved yourself and are truly ready for marriage. Then when you know that the person is the one, have talked with a pastor, and attended pre-marital counseling classes, you can walk down the wedding runner. And God will bless that aspect of your relationship in an awesome way.

When I spoke on this subject in church, a couple that was test-driving took this challenge seriously and moved out until their marriage. When I spoke with them later, they urged me to highlight this point and emphasize how critical this move was to their future relationship together.

GOD'S RELATIONAL ROAD SIGNS

Other signs along the way also need our attention. I call these relational road signs. And defective daters are notorious for disregarding and failing to observe these signs. On my way to church one Sunday, I stopped at a stop sign and a truck beside me just flew through it. Fortunately, this reckless behavior did not cause an accident. But if you don't observe the road signs of life, you have a high likelihood of getting into a serious relational wreck.

Speed Zone Ahead

The first sign that singles must observe is the Speed

Limit sign. I say this often to singles in my church and will say it again here—go slow and get to know. Wait at least a year until you marry. Here is some great information, the 411, on taking it slow and being patient. I can tell you from experience that the extra time that peels off the clock will either give you more confidence or erode your confidence concerning the vehicle of marriage. It is so important to wait and to evaluate your feelings and commitment to both your potential mate and to marriage.

So many get married too young and too rapidly. A recent study by the federal government regarding women and marriage concluded that the older a woman is at first marriage, the longer that marriage is likely to last. Women who get married young are almost twice as likely to divorce than those who wait until their late twenties and early thirties. Many relational experts believe that it is best for single adults to get married after they are twenty-eight years of age. They assert that, because the period of adolescence is longer in modern times, most people are not mature enough until they are at least twenty-five.

When I think about going slow, I think about Genesis 29 and Jacob's relationship with Rachel. Jacob met Rachel and he was immediately attracted to her; he knew he wanted to marry her. One day he kissed Rachel and afterwards just started weeping. You can read it for yourself. That must have been some kiss. Then Jacob asked Rachel's father for her hand in marriage. Rachel's father said that he could have her, but first he needed to work for him for seven years.

Genesis 29:20 says, "So Jacob served seven years to get Rachel, but they seemed like only a few days to him because of his love for her." I am going to direct my three daughters' future boyfriends to this text. And then, after the first seven years of waiting, the Bible says that Rachel's father tricked Jacob into marrying her sister, and he had to wait an additional seven years before he could finally marry Rachel. A minimum of one year of dating and waiting for marriage is starting to sound pretty good, isn't it?

Don't Be Afraid to Stop

This next sign is going to take some guts to observe. It's the Stop Sign. I can't tell you what to do because I am not you. But if you have a check in your spirit, if you see some warning lights or some baggage that hasn't been dealt with, have the guts to stop. If it doesn't feel right, stop. "Well, Ed, the invitations have been sent out." Stop. "My friends are pressuring me." Stop. "He is rich." Stop. Don't be hesitant to do that because you are talking about a decision for life, a forever commitment.

Make a U-Turn

Whenever you hear the term repent in the Bible, it means to do a U-Turn, to go the opposite way, to do a 180. I love this symbol, because it illustrates what God does. God tells me that when I just begin to turn, He is there to greet me, to save me and to change me. He doesn't wait for me to go all they way. No, He is meeting me by the curve of the U, and that gives me confidence. It should give you confidence too.

A lot of defective daters need to come clean and say, "I have messed up. I have a lot of dating flaws in my life. I want to do a U-Turn and begin to do this stuff God's way. I want to drive on His street, between His guardrails, and on His autobahn. I don't want to go off-road. I want to really understand and process this biblical perspective on spouse selection." Good for you. All you have got to do is begin to turn the car and God will be right there.

Yield the Right of Way

The Yield Sign is shaped like arms outstretched to God

in a yielding position. That should be our posture before God. We become a Christian by saying, "God, have your way in my life. I receive Christ into my life." And we become an effective dater when we say, "God, take the right of way on this dating journey. I give all of my desire for the opposite sex and all of my baggage to you. I want to go Your way." When you do that, you will meet your Ulti-Mate. And it will be a lot better than driving a Mercedes 500SL.

CHAPTER
4

DANGEROUS BINDS
Maintaining Purity in the Midst of Passion

When I was a teenager, I became fascinated with a very dangerous sport—shark fishing from the shoreline. The thrill of landing one of these deep water predators was one thing I thought that I just had to experience. So one weekend a few brave buddies and I ventured down to Galveston Island, Texas to attempt the unimaginable in my mother's mind; we were off to catch a shark.

We came up with an interesting technique in order to catch one of these beasts. Because our big game rod and reel was too big to cast into the water, one guy would stand on the beach with the rod and reel and a second guy would bait the end of the line with the shark's favorite food—a bloody stingray. Then the third guy, who had to be a little bit crazy to complete his task, would take the bloody stingray, put it in a rubber dinghy, and motor out about a half mile off shore while the guy on the beach fed him line. When the guy in the rubber dinghy got a half mile off shore, he would throw the shark bait overboard and head back to shore.

The first night, I was elected to be the one to head out in the dinghy. And to be completely candid, I was scared out of my wits. I would be heading out into the night with who knows what lurking under my craft. But I didn't want the other guys to know, so I went out in the dinghy like it was no big deal. When I got out far enough from shore I threw the bloody stingray into the water. I watched it slowly settle into the coffee black waters of the Gulf of Mexico and then turned around to start up the Sears outboard, 2.5 horsepower motor to head back to land. The blood in the area had begun to attract the sharks and the last thing I wanted was for the stingray to be an appetizer for their main course—me!

To my horror, the engine quit just as I tried to start it. In the eerie silence, I peered down into the abyss and could see my worst nightmare developing before my eyes. Sharks were beginning to circle, and I couldn't leave the area. The shark line had gotten entangled in the motor! And dangling dangerously about three feet below the little raft was a bloody stingray.

Now I want you to get the picture of this scenario. I am in a rubber raft with a plywood bottom, a bloody stingray is dangling under the raft and my buddy is on the beach with the rod and reel—that I am hooked to! Basically, I was a human fishing cork. I was in a dangerous bind, a very dangerous bind.

A lot of single people are in dangerous binds right now. You may not be tangled up in shark lines off the coast of Galveston, but you are tangled in the binds of premarital sex. And the Bible has a lot to say about this dangerous premarital sex bind. God says many times, both directly and indirectly, that we are to abstain from sex until marriage.

FOR OUR OWN GOOD

Now, when I make a comment like that, the typical response is not, "Ed, thank you so much for showing me the error of my ways. I'm so glad that I understand God's view on sex now. I'm so happy that I have to wait until marriage for sexual intercourse."

No, most singles have a different reaction. It's more like, "What! Why is God raining on my sexual parade? Here God arbitrarily decides that those who are single have to abstain from sex and those who are married have a blank check?! That is so unfair. I don't understand it. And I certainly don't like it!"

Singles who think this way fail to see the why behind God's prohibition. They fail to see that God has given us this directive for our own good. We need to look at God's command from his perspective, not our own. So for just a minute, let's consider all that God does for our own good.

We are made in His image—for our own good. We are the crown of His creation—for our own good. He has given us the Bible for guidance—for our own good. And He has given us the church for encouragement and support—for our own good. Do you see a pattern here?

But then He comes along and tells us to wait until marriage to have sex? Yes. And it too is...for our own good. You see, we cannot break God's laws without suffering consequences. And when we choose to ignore God's command of no sex before marriage, we are going to face some serious consequences.

It Builds a Barrier

The first consequence of premarital sex is that it

builds a barrier. Isaiah 59:2 says, "Your iniquities have separated you from your God; your sins have hidden his face from you, so that he will not hear." In Psalm 66:18 David says, "If I had cherished sin in my heart, the Lord would not have listened."

As a believer, what happened to David's life when he was involved in sexual sin? A barrier was built between himself and God. And David could not reach his full potential until that barrier between himself and God was torn down, until David began to follow God's commandments.

When a barrier is present between yourself and another party you can't communicate, you can't fellowship, and you can't truly connect with that person. Premarital sex builds one of those barriers between God and us. And those barriers keep adding up until they finally result in a domino effect in our lives.

As a child, I remember watching Johnny Carson on television almost every Friday night. One of my favorite episodes was a night that he had a man on the show who attempted to break the world record for the longest chain of dominos. This guy had lined up what seemed to me like miles and miles of dominos. After he had the whole thing set up, Johnny walked out and pushed over the first domino. It started a chain reaction that went for several minutes. Finally, the last domino fell and Johnny announced, "Congratulations! You have just broken the world record!"

Sexual sin is a lot like those falling dominos. Only with sin there is no room for congratulations at the end. Premarital sex will kick start a domino effect in your life that can ultimately lead to spiritual ruin.

- The first domino to be pushed over is sexual intercourse outside of the marriage bed.

- The second falling domino is guilt. The Holy Spirit begins to convict you—you know that you were wrong.

- After guilt comes the domino of self-deception. You are deceived into thinking that everything is A-OK. You tell yourself, "Everybody is doing it. After all, this is the twenty-first century."

- The next domino is desertion. You become cold and apathetic; you begin to turn your back on God and the church. And then the dominos continue to fall. If enough dominoes fall you can become so distant from God that your impact and influence for Christ hits bottom. And that's exactly where the evil one wants us to be.

Am I saying that sexual sin leads to eternal destruction and separation from God? No. Our God is a loving and merciful God who will never let his children go. If we have accepted Christ's gift of forgiveness, our eternal destiny is safe and secure in his hands. But choosing to continually disobey His commands will lead to a life devoid of his presence. We can choose to turn away from Him, and in doing so lose out on the abundant life he wants for us right now.

It is a pipe dream to believe that you can have authentic fellowship with God and be involved in premarital sex. You can't do it. That math doesn't work.

If we are going to really understand God's design for sexuality, we have to look at it within the context of being created in the image of God. When God made man, He stamped on him His masculine character qualities. When God made female, He stamped on her the feminine character qualities of His personality. Thus, when a man and a woman come together in the act of sex within the context of marriage, the total image of God is coming together in its masculine and feminine aspects—the way God intended and designed it.

That is why the Bible tells us that the equation

of marriage is: 1 + 1 = 1. It is two becoming one—a cohesiveness, a blending, a cleaving. Sex acts like Super Glue as it bonds two people together.

Thus, when we have sexual intercourse outside of marriage, we are making a mockery of the very image of God. God wants His image to be formed in our lives. He wants the act of sex to be done strictly in the context of the lifelong covenant of marriage; not in the back seat of some car—not because you are engaged; and not because you say you really love the guy or girl.

> **THE EQUATION OF MARRIAGE IS: 1 + 1 = 1. IT IS TWO BECOMING ONE—A COHESIVENESS, A BLENDING, A CLEAVING. SEX ACTS LIKE SUPER GLUE AS IT BONDS TWO PEOPLE TOGETHER.**

Simply stated, premarital sex is called fornication in the Bible. I defined that in a previous chapter. And the term sexual immorality includes sexual activity leading up to the point of intercourse. 1 Thessalonians 4:3 tells us, "Avoid sexual immorality." So, not only should we avoid sexual intercourse, we should keep from doing those things that lead inevitably to it.

I want you to notice something. Every time God gives us a freedom, He puts that freedom within the perimeter of a fence. He gives us sex as a gift, but He says that it must be practiced only under His directives. He tells us to stay within His fence. But the moment we jump that fence and think we can do sex our own way, we are going to get into trouble. Sure, everything may seem okay for awhile. But one day we will wake up and experience pain, alienation, and separation like we can't imagine.

God loves you and me so much that He wants to spare us from all of that. And he also wants us to experience the pleasure of sex within his perimeters. I love what C.S. Lewis once said. "Pleasure is God's invention, not the devil's."

But if you are having sex outside of the marriage bed, for the most part you are using that other person. You are using that person for your own pleasure and basically showing that person that you want the sex without having to make the commitment. In the process, though, you are missing out on the real pleasure God intended sex to bring within a committed, sanctified relationship. You are settling for a counterfeit instead of the real thing.

Now, some people may read this and say, "Okay, I'm supposed to avoid sexual immorality. But I'm engaged. My fiancé and I know that we are going to get married, so it's okay for us to go ahead and have sex." In my twenty years of marriage and ministry, I have yet to find any conditional clauses to God's commandment. There are no amendments guaranteeing the right to have sex while you are engaged. The Bible communicates clearly that we are not to have sex before marriage—not tonight; not Homecoming night; not prom night; not engagement night; not any night. Premarital sex builds barriers.

It Fillets Feelings

There is another dangerous bind to premarital sex. Not only does it build barriers in our lives, it also fillets feelings. It acts like a razor sharp Buck knife and cuts right through the feelings we have.

When my son E.J. was five years old he found out that I kept two Buck knives on the top shelf of my closet. When he saw them he asked me if he could hold one of them. I told him that he could, but that we would have to leave the blade folded because it was dangerous. He held the knife and thought it was one of the greatest things he'd ever done. And almost every day for a few weeks he would come in and ask if he could hold the knife.

After a while, I began to see that holding the knife with the blade folded wasn't as exciting for him as it had been at first. Then he asked if he could see the knife with the blade out. I thought to myself, "He's old enough to learn about how to hold a knife properly. He's really mature for his age. Besides, I'm right here with him. What could go wrong?"

So, I decided to show him how to hold the knife with the blade out. Just as I was showing him, he reached up and grabbed the knife by the blade. You can imagine my horror in those few seconds as I watched my only son grasping a razor sharp blade in his little palm.

I calmly told him to release the blade, to unclench his grip. After a second or two, he slowly released his grip and I gently took the knife from his hand. Now, when he grew a little older, I showed him the proper way to hold a knife. Obviously, he was too young when he was five. But he was smart enough to release the knife when directed to by his father, whom he trusts.

Sexuality is a lot like that Buck knife. Many of us take our sexuality and we hold it and grasp it tightly, not realizing that we are white-knuckling a razor sharp blade that has the potential to do us great harm. We say that it is ours, that we can do as we please, that we can do sex our own way. But God says, "Give me the knife. Give me your sexuality." And if we refuse to follow his way, if we insist on holding it too tightly, sex will wound, scar, maim and fillet our feelings for life.

God is simply telling us, "Unclench the white-knuckle grip you have on your sexuality. Give it to me and let me show you how to use it." And once God takes it, He will show us that this gift is awesome, far beyond description when it is used in the loving commitment of marriage.

Sex is not just a physical thing. That is why you can't do it with somebody and just walk away. It is not one-dimensional. It is multifaceted and multi-dimensional. There is a spiritual aspect to it, an emotional aspect to it, and a psychological aspect to it. It acts as an adhesive between two people, a bonding agent stronger than anything else.

So many breakups are overly dramatic and traumatic because of the practice of premarital sex within the relationship. Much more than just a physical link is at stake with sex. When the people break up and stop dating, some serious feelings need to be dealt with and let go—emotional connections are being severed, spiritual bonds are being split, and psychological ties are being cut.

But again, our loving God wants to spare us from this pain and suffering. He says that it hurts Him to see people who matter to Him dealing with scars and wounds and filleted feelings all because they were involved in sex outside of the marriage bed.

IT RUINS RELATIONSHIPS

The third danger or consequence of premarital sex is that it ruins relationships. A dating relationship is all about courtship. It is a time when you should develop communication, intimacy, spiritual core values, and even conflict-resolution with the other person. All of this is vital work that must be done during the courtship phase in order to provide a strong base for a lasting lifelong relationship.

But when you get involved in premarital sex, you pole vault over all the important aspects of courtship. You bypass those foundational facets of dating because you want to get to the thrills, the chills, and the electricity of sex. Thus, you retard and stymie the relationship's ability to grow. And just like a pole vaulter falling into the pit after each vault, premarital sex leads to a relational pit. Every time you vault over real relational growth, the bar gets set higher and higher and the longer the fall is into the pit.

Take advantage of the time you have during the dating and courtship period to work on the difficult stuff. And once you get the hard stuff right, if you feel led to get married, then sex will only deepen that relationship. Sex will help keep a beautiful thing—your marriage—beautiful. But don't pole vault over the important stuff. It can ruin your relationship.

S.T.D.s

We know that S.T.D.s, sexually transmitted diseases, are a tragic reality in our world today—AIDS, syphilis, gonorrhea, herpes, etc. And we know that a person runs a risk of contracting one of these diseases every time he or she has sex outside of marriage. But there is an S.T.D. that every single person involved in premarital sex has already contracted, and they don't even know it. It is a "Stupid Thinking Disorder."

Sex is so powerful that when you lock into someone with sex, it automatically gives you the stupid thinking disorder. It destroys your discernment. You can't tell if this person is truly right for you or not. Because you pole vaulted over the difficult aspects of a relationship, you never really know if you can work together on them. And it all stems from the power of sex.

Most experts agree that sex alone can bond two people and hold them together for three to five years.

What happens after those three or five years? Well, go back to the beginning of this scenario.

You started out dating. You went out maybe three or four times, and then jumped right to sex. And for a few months, the sex was hot and heavy—everything seemed to be working out great. The time moved ahead and you decided to marry this person. Keep in mind you had already pole vaulted over the difficult areas of the relationship up to that point. Then three to five years later you wake up and wonder what you did. You say to yourself, "I messed up. I didn't realize this person dealt with conflict that way. I didn't know that they were driven by such different motivations that I am. Where did I go wrong? And what do I do now? This is not the person I thought I was getting involved with!"

What happened? The power of sex happened. You paid the high price of promiscuity and your relationship was ruined. But there is a very simple solution to avoiding that situation. Don't get involved in premarital sex. Save yourself for you spouse. Wait until marriage. There is an interesting phenomenon when it comes to relationships. Most men will endure some "relationship stuff" just for the sex. And many women will endure the sex just for the relationship stuff.

It's almost humorous to watch the different reactions that single men and single women have when I speak about premarital sex. Women typically nod their heads and say, "That's right, Ed. We should wait. It's way too important to deal with flippantly!" And the guys sit there quietly saying to themselves, "Oh, man, this is a joke! I can handle sex. After all, it's just sex—it's fun!" I realize that those are broad-brush statements, but you get the point.

I know how difficult this area is—after all, we are sexual beings. Virginity is a past tense thing for many, many people. But I don't care where you are in this realm, there is some wonderful news for you. We serve a God who will give you another chance. We serve a God who will break down those barriers. We serve a God who will heal those filleted feelings. We serve a God who will restore ruined relationships.

If you humbly go before God and ask for another chance, a chance to do it His way, He will grant you that opportunity. But going to God is not something that anyone can do for you. You have got to do it yourself. You have got to take care of the business between you and God. You've got to make that choice.

I kind of left you dangling with the shark story I began earlier in the chapter. You must be wondering, "Did he get away? What happened?" Well, I'll tell you what happened.

As I was bobbing up and down like a human fishing

cork in the water, I knew I was in trouble. Any number of things could have happened: the razor sharp hooks from the line could have come up and punctured the raft; the waves could have knocked over the flimsy raft; or the sharks could have bitten right through the dinghy.

I was half a mile off shore and if I fell in, there was little hope of escaping. So I did something radical. I put the big game shark line in my mouth and I bit through it. It was tough and my gums started bleeding. But I bit right through it. And when I did, I freed myself from the stingray and the little raft began to float with the current. To keep from floating out to sea, I had to take my little K-Mart paddle and paddle against the current. After about an hour of intense paddling, I finally made it to the shore of safety.

If you are involved in the dangerous binds of premarital sex, it is time you do something radical. It is time for you to break the line that entangles you. It won't be easy. But God will give you the strength. Be prepared, though. Once you get unbound, you will feel the currents of our culture begin to take you back out to sea. You will feel the waves of sensuality rising up.

But I challenge you to paddle against the current of our culture. Row and row and row. Keep yourself pure against the pull of passion, until you reach the shores of sexual purity. And then stay there until marriage. It will be one of the greatest foundations and feelings in your life. From this day forward remain pure until you are able to say, before friends, family, and God, those two life changing covenant words: "I do."

As we end this book, I need to ask a crucial question: While you are waiting for mating, are you rating your dating God's way? If you will make a commitment to do that, I promise that when you are ready for marriage every aspect of your relationship, including sexual intimacy, will be a beautiful thing. Remember, God has given you these relational parameters because He loves you. Demonstrate your love for Him by your obedience, trusting that he has your best interest at heart in dating, in mating, and in every other aspect of your life.

> **WHILE YOU ARE WAITING FOR MATING, ARE YOUR RATING YOUR DATING GOD'S WAY?**

ENDNOTES

Chapter 2

1. divorcemag.com
2. divorceinfo.com
3. George Barna, Transforming Your Children Into Spiritual Champions (Ventura, CA: Regal Books, 2003, 23.)

Other books by Ed Young available on EdYoung.com:

Beauty Full
Becoming More Than Just Pretty

Each year, society spends billions of dollars to convince us that beauty is exactly skin deep. But when we value physical looks more than the soul, we drain beauty of its full potential. In these pages, you will find the cure the world so often promises but never delivers. And you will see that your God-given beauty is as close as your heart, as deep as your soul.

Outrageous, Contagious Joy
Five Big Questions to Help You Discover One Great Life

What if there was more to life than you ever thought possible? Something beyond your wildest dreams? What if you could have a bigger, more meaningful life right now?

Created to help you think about where you are and where you are going, this remarkable book will give you very specific and practical steps that will revolutionize the way you think of —and carry out—your life.

You!
The Journey to the Center of Your Worth

The answer to reaching your greatest potential lies in this God-centered approach to the journey to the center of your worth. In this meaningful book, you will quickly discover that you are God's treasure—divinely loved, cherished, and chosen—and encounter a whole new view of YOU!

The Creative Marriage
The Art of Keeping Your Love Alive

Disposable relationships and throw away marriages permeate our culture. When the dream fades and the realities of life set in, many just throw in the towel. In their book, The Creative Marriage: The Art of Keeping Your Love Alive, Ed and Lisa Young take a penetrating look at what it means to have a lasting marriage in today's world. After more than twenty years of marriage, they speak openly and honestly about the hard work involved in a creative marriage and the lasting rewards of doing it God's way.

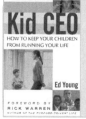

Kid CEO
How to Keep Your Children From Running Your Life

Through a thought-provoking yet entertaining analysis of contemporary family dynamics, Ed Young challenges parents to reclaim their leadership role and explains why marriage must take first priority in the home.

These and many other series are available on CD and DVD at EdYoung.com:

Love Affair

Marriage is designed by God to be a lifelong covenant, a forever love affair. But how do we keep that covenant from being threatened by another kind of affair? This explosive series by Ed Young teaches us how to protect our marriages and families from adultery--how to keep the unthinkable from tearing apart the marital love affair.

Sexual Revolution

It's time to put the bed back in church and church back in the bed. In this series, Ed Young helps us get back to God's incredible design for sex, beginning with the important realization that He created this life-uniting gift. Focusing on when to, how to, and who to enjoy sex with, this powerful teaching promises to revolutionize your perspective on sex.

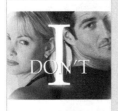

I Don't for Singles

Every married couple says two words that will change their lives forever: "I Do." But before the "I Dos," we need to remember the "I Don'ts." In this contemporary series on relationships, Ed Young considers the things we don't do before and after marriage that make all the difference in the lasting impact of the marital vows.

RPMs: Recognizing Potential Mates

Whether you're a single adult, a student, or a parent, this creatively driven series of talks will provide foundational principles on how to date and select a mate God's way. We're going to cruise past the cultural myths and embark on a supercharged ride to the ultimate relational destination.

Just Lust

Men and women alike, no one escapes its insidious influence. God calls it the lust of the flesh and it has the power to enslave and destroy everyone it touches. In this hard-hitting series of talks, Ed Young provides a strategy for spiritual survival in a culture of lust.